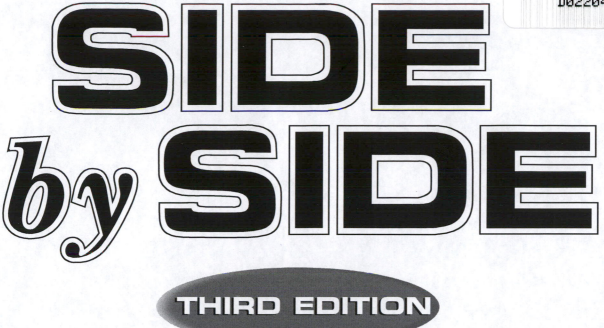

SIDE by SIDE

THIRD EDITION

Testing Program 2

Steven J. Molinsky
Bill Bliss

Contributing Author

Robert Doherty

Longman

longman.com

Printed in The United States Of America

Side by Side Testing Program 2, 3rd edition

Copyright © 2003 by Prentice Hall Regents
Addison Wesley Longman, Inc.
A Pearson Education Company.
All rights reserved.

Pearson Education, 10 Bank Street, White Plains, NY 10606

Vice president, director of publishing: *Allen Ascher*
Editorial manager: *Pam Fishman*
Vice president, director of design and production: *Rhea Banker*
Associate director of electronic production: *Aliza Greenblatt*
Production manager: *Ray Keating*
Director of manufacturing: *Patrice Fraccio*
Associate digital layout manager: *Paula D. Williams*
Interior design: *Paula D. Williams*
Cover design: *Monika Popwitz*

Illustrator: *Richard E. Hill*

The authors gratefully acknowledge the contribution
of Tina Carver in the development of the original
Side by Side program.

ISBN 0-13-026768-6 NB2I

Student's Name _____   I.D. Number _____

Course _____   Teacher _____   Date _____

CHOOSE

Example:

Robert _____.

- a. like to cook
- **(b.)** likes to cook
- c. like cook
- d. likes cook

1. My sister _____ TV.

- a. don't like to watch
- b. like to watch
- c. doesn't like watch
- d. doesn't like to watch

2. My children and I _____ adventure movies.

- a. like see
- b. likes to see
- c. like
- d. don't like see

3. What_____ do on the weekend?

- a. you like to
- b. do you like to
- c. you do like to
- d. do you like

4. I don't like _____ very much.

- a. listen to popular music
- b. rock music
- c. skate
- d. to rock music

5. Ted and Howard _____ the subway.

- a. don't like to take
- b. don't like to take to
- c. doesn't like to take
- d. don't like take

CHOOSE

Example:

My parents gave _____ a bicycle for my birthday.

   a. I
   (b.) me
   c. my
   d. you

6. I can't give _____ a CD player.

   a. me
   b. his
   c. him
   d. us

7. What did Susan's husband give _____ for her birthday?

   a. her
   b. she
   c. him
   d. me

8. Helen gave _____ a painting for their anniversary.

   a. they
   b. our
   c. their
   d. them

9. Mary and James gave _____ a very nice plant.

   a. we
   b. our
   c. us
   d. my

10. What _____ her last year?

   a. did you gave
   b. did you give
   c. you gave
   d. do you give

CHOOSE

Example:

Tim _____ his car every day.

a. going to wash
b. washing
(c.) washes
d. wash

11. My wife and I _____ dancing last weekend.

a. are going
b. went
c. go
d. did

12. Is Maria going to _____ spaghetti tomorrow?

a. cooks
b. cooked
c. cook
d. to cook

13. I _____ mathematics every Sunday.

a. studying
b. going to study
c. am studying
d. study

14. He _____ his car last year.

a. is going to sell
b. is selling
c. sold
d. sells

15. Jimmy and Patty _____ right now.

a. are swimming
b. swam
c. swim
d. swimming

16. Our family _____ to the beach every summer.

a. is going
b. go
c. likes go
d. goes

17. We _____ the house tomorrow.

a. go to clean
b. are going to clean
c. want clean
d. cleaned

18. Her friends gave her flowers, but she _____ a watch.

a. wanting
b. is going to want
c. wanted
d. gave

19. His parents _____ TV last night.

a. watched
b. are watching
c. watches
d. watch

20. Nancy isn't home. _____ her bicycle now.

a. She rides
b. She rode
c. She's riding
d. She riding

WHICH WORD?

Amy and Tom [(are)   our   is] very good friends. They [go   studied   went][21]

to college together a few years ago, and now they [work   working   worked][22] together.

Tomorrow is Amy's birthday. [Next   Last   In this][23] year Tom gave Amy a sweater, but

this year he's going to give [her   them   him][24] a novel because she

[like to   likes   likes to][25] read.

Score: _____

Student's Name _____ I.D. Number _____

Course _____ Teacher _____ Date _____

CHOOSE

Example:

    A. How much milk do you want?
    B. _____.
        a. How much.
       (b.) Not too much.
        c. Too much.
        d. Not too many

1. A. How many cookies do you want?
     B. _____.
        a. Not too much.
        b. How many.
        c. Not too many.
        d. Too much.

2. A. How do you like the cheese?
     B. I think _____ delicious.
        a. it
        b. they're
        c. their
        d. it's

3. A. How much yogurt do you want?
     B. Just _____.
        a. a little
        b. too much
        c. a few
        d. too many

4. A. How do you like the eggs?
     B. I think _____ delicious.
        a. they
        b. they're
        c. their
        d. it's

5. A. These french fries are delicious.
     B. I'm glad _____.
        a. you like it
        b. they like you
        c. you like them
        d. they're french fries

CHOOSE

Example:

_____ meatballs do you want?

a. Not too many
b. How many *(circled)*
c. Too many
d. How much

6. She drinks _____ coffee.

a. not too many
b. too much
c. just little
d. too many

7. I made the rice. I'm glad _____ .

a. it's just a little
b. you like them
c. they're delicious
d. you like it

8. _____ oranges do you want?

a. How many
b. Too many
c. Not too many
d. How much

9. _____ any mayonnaise.

a. Let's make
b. There aren't
c. There isn't
d. How many

10. I eat _____ bananas every day.

a. too much
b. a few
c. a little
d. just many

CHOOSE

Example:

There aren't any _____ .

a. tea
b. lemons *(circled)*
c. cake
d. rice

11. There isn't any _____ .

a. ketchup
b. potatoes
c. onions
d. sandwich

12. There aren't any _____ .

a. bread
b. butter
c. eggs
d. spaghetti

13. There isn't any _____ .

a. pears
b. meatballs
c. tomatoes
d. orange juice

14. There aren't any _____ .

a. fish
b. bananas
c. mustard
d. apple pie

15. There isn't any _____ .

a. carrots
b. grapes
c. lettuce
d. apples

CHOOSE

Example:

   A. Where's the salt?
   B. _____ on the table.
     (a.) It's
     b. They're
     c. It
     d. There isn't

16. A. Where's the salad?
     B. _____ in the dining room.
      a. A little
      b. They're
      c. It's
      d. How much

17. A. Where's the _____?
     B. It's in the refrigerator.
      a. cabinet
      b. cheese
      c. sandwiches
      d. table

18. A. Where are the hamburgers?
     B. _____ on the counter.
      a. Not too many
      b. Are they
      c. It's
      d. They're

19. A. Where's the sugar?
     B. It's on the _____.
      a. table
      b. refrigerator
      c. freezer
      d. lemonade

20. A. I can't find the soy sauce.
     B. _____ in the refrigerator.
      a. Let's make some
      b. Is
      c. They're
      d. It's

WHAT'S THE WORD?

much	they	it	them	is	are

Albert doesn't like vegetables. In fact, he never eats _____**them**_____. His wife tells him that

vegetables _____**21**_____ good for him, but Albert doesn't think so. He thinks _____**22**_____

taste terrible.

Albert's wife likes pizza. In fact, she eats _____**23**_____ all the time. Albert tells her she

eats too _____**24**_____ pizza, but she doesn't think so. She thinks that pizza _____**25**_____

delicious.

Score: _____

Student's Name _____	I.D. Number _____
Course _____	Teacher _____	Date _____

CHOOSE

Example:

I need a _____ of soup.

  ⓐ can
  b. bag
  c. bunch
  d. pound

1. We need two _____ of bread.

  a. loafs
  b. loaves
  c. jars
  d. bunches

2. I need a _____ of lettuce.

  a. quart
  b. box
  c. head
  d. pint

3. They need a _____ of meat.

  a. pound
  b. bag
  c. bottle
  d. bunch

4. I need a _____ of cheese.

  a. gallon
  b. pint
  c. quart
  d. half pound

5. We need a _____ eggs.

  a. dozen of
  b. bag of
  c. dozen
  d. bunch

CHOOSE

Example:

_____ any more lettuce.

(a.) There isn't
b. There aren't
c. Is there
d. How much is

6. _____ any more hot chocolate.

a. Do we need
b. There isn't
c. I recommend
d. There aren't

7. _____ any more strawberries?

a. We need
b. Aren't
c. Are
d. Are there

8. _____ any more bottles of ketchup.

a. There aren't
b. We have to buy
c. Are
d. There isn't

9. _____ any more fish.

a. Add
b. Do we need
c. There isn't
d. There aren't

10. _____ any more rice?

a. Please give me
b. Is there
c. How much is
d. Are there

CHOOSE

Example:

I recommend the pie. _____ excellent.

(a.) It's
b. They're
c. Is it
d. Everybody likes it

11. I recommend the pancakes. Everybody says _____.

a. it's magnificent
b. they're an order
c. they're wonderful
d. they're for breakfast

12. Do you want _____ milk?

a. a dish of
b. a glass of
c. piece of
d. glass of

13. I suggest the chocolate ice cream. _____.

a. It's delicious.
b. They're out of this world.
c. I can't decide it.
d. Everybody says it's dessert.

14. _____ the nuts?

a. I recommend
b. How is
c. How many
d. How are

15. Please give me a _____ apple pie.

a. more
b. bowl
c. piece of
d. cup of

CHOOSE

Example:

_____ butter into the saucepan.

a. Slice a few
b. Bake a little
c. Put a little *(circled)*
d. Add a few

16. _____ onions.

a. Pour few
b. Chop up a few
c. Mix as little
d. Chop up a little

17. Add _____.

a. a few rice
b. a little raisins
c. a little salt
d. for two hours

18. Put _____ sugar into a bowl.

a. a few cups of
b. a little cup
c. a little of
d. a few cups

19. _____ a little water.

a. Cut up
b. Slice
c. Chop
d. Pour in

20. _____ honey.

a. Pour in a few
b. Add a little
c. Cut up a little
d. Add a few

WHAT'S THE WORD?

of	much	is	It	lot	pint

A. How _____much_____ does a _____21_____ _____22_____ ice cream cost?

B. _____23_____ costs four ninety-nine.

A. That's a _____24_____ of money!

B. You're right. Ice cream _____25_____ very expensive this week.

Score: _____

Student's Name _____ I.D. Number _____

Course _____ Teacher _____ Date _____

CHOOSE

Example:

A. Will the game begin soon?
B. Yes, _____.
    a. he will
    b. we will
    (c.) it will
    d. will it

1. A. Will Lucy be ready soon?
    B. Yes. _____ ready in a few minutes.
        a. She's
        b. She be
        c. She'll be
        d. She's be

2. A. Will your brother return soon?
    B. No, _____.
        a. he'll won't
        b. he'll return soon
        c. he's won't
        d. he won't

3. A. Will the books arrive soon?
    B. Yes. _____ arrive at 5:00.
        a. They'll
        b. There
        c. Their
        d. They're

4. A. Will Jill get out of the hospital soon?
    B. _____.
        a. No, she'll won't.
        b. No, she won't.
        c. Yes, she'll will.
        d. Yes, she won't.

5. A. Will you get your driver's license soon?
    B. Yes. _____ get it in a week.
        a. Will
        b. I won't
        c. I'll
        d. I'm

WHEN?

Example:

The train will arrive in _____.

a. a little week
(b.) an hour
c. seven o'clock
d. 7:30

6. The guests will be here in a few _____.

a. while
b. hour
c. minutes
d. half an hour

7. The game will begin at _____.

a. half an hour
b. ten o'clock
c. soon
d. ten minutes

8. It'll end _____.

a. ten minutes
b. hours
c. a little while
d. next week

9. I'll be there _____.

a. soon
b. at a few days
c. half an hour
d. five o'clock

10. We'll get home in two or three _____.

a. while
b. o'clock
c. hours
d. week

CHOOSE

Example:

Put on your helmet! You might _____.

a. catch a cold
b. have a terrible time
(c.) hurt your head
d. hit

11. Put on your safety glasses! You might _____.

a. hit your eyes
b. hurt your eyes
c. get hurt your eyes
d. see

12. Gary doesn't want to go skiing. He might _____.

a. drown
b. get seasick
c. break his leg
d. fall asleep

13. Watch your step! You might _____.

a. step on your feet
b. fall asleep
c. get sick
d. fall

14. My son is sick. He might _____.

a. be the flu
b. have the measles
c. feel terrible
d. be pregnant

15. Don't touch those wires! You might _____.

a. get a shock
b. have a terrible time
c. get a sunburn
d. get hit your head

CHOOSE

Example:

I don't know. Maybe _____ clean it tomorrow.

a. I'll (circled)
b. I might
c. I'll might
d. I

16. I'm not sure. Maybe it will, and maybe it _____.

a. might
b. can't
c. won't
d. isn't

17. I'm afraid I _____ have a terrible time.

a. won't
b. might
c. don't
d. might not

18. I'm afraid we _____ come to your party this weekend.

a. might
b. can
c. will
d. can't

19. _____ return soon?

a. Will he
b. Will he might
c. Is he going
d. Do you think he

20. We aren't sure. _____ go to a museum.

a. We'll
b. We might
c. Maybe
d. We'll might

WHICH WORD?

A. Hello. This is Lucy Randall. I'm afraid | (I can't)   I'll   I might | come to work.

I think I | will   won't   might |²¹ have the flu.

B. That's too bad. | Will you   Are you   Can you |²² going to go to a clinic?

A. I think I | sure   so   might |²³ .

B. | Will   Don't   Do |²⁴ you be at work tomorrow?

A. I'm not sure. I | will   might   won't |²⁵ not go to work tomorrow either.

Score: _____

CHOOSE

Example:

My old bicycle was fast, but my new bicycle _____.

a. is more fast
b. is faster
c. was faster
d. was more faster

(b. circled)

1. I think the streets here are _____ than the streets in Los Angeles.

   a. more wide
   b. more wider
   c. wider
   d. more long

2. You should buy that dress for Sally's wedding. It's _____.

   a. more fancer
   b. fancier
   c. more fancier
   d. fancer

3. Richard's old girlfriend was intelligent, but his new girlfriend is _____.

   a. more intelligenter
   b. intelligenter
   c. more smarter
   d. smarter

4. They think their dog is _____ than our dog, but I don't.

   a. cuter
   b. more cuter
   c. cuteer
   d. more cuteer

5. I'm going to vote for Gary Gray. He's _____ than Gregory Green.

   a. more honest
   b. honester
   c. honest
   d. more honester

6. Miguel's pronunciation is good, but Maria's pronunciation is _____.

   a. more good
   b. better
   c. gooder
   d. more better

7. These flowers are pretty, but those flowers are _____.

   a. more pretty
   b. more prettier
   c. pretty
   d. prettier

8. Is their car _____ than our car?

   a. bigger
   b. attractiver
   c. biger
   d. more attractiver

9. The desktop computer is _____ than the notebook computer.

    a. expensiver

    b. powerfuler

    c. more powerful

    d. more expensiver

10. Our children are _____ than their children.

    a. more nice

    b. more polite

    c. politer

    d. more politer

CHOOSE

Example:

    Your dog is friendlier _____.

    a. than mine dog

    (b.) than mine

    c. as mine

    d. as my dog

11. I think our daughter is much more talented _____.

    a. their daughter

    b. as theirs

    c. as their daughter

    d. than theirs

12. The Bradleys' new dishwasher isn't as quiet _____.

    a. as ours

    b. as us

    c. as we are

    d. ours

13. Pam's computer is more reliable _____.

    a. as her

    b. than his

    c. as his

    d. than him

14. My geography teacher isn't _____.

    a. as smart as mine

    b. as smarter than yours

    c. as smart as yours

    d. as smarter as yours

15. Mr. Brown's cake is more delicious _____.

    a. as him

    b. than her

    c. than him

    d. than hers

OPINIONS

Example:

    A. Bob isn't as handsome as Bill.

    B. I agree. _____.

       (a.) Bill is more handsome than Bob.

       b. Bob is more handsome than Bill.

       c. Bill is as handsome as Bob.

16. A. My briefcase isn't as attractive as Susan's briefcase.

    B. I disagree. I think _____.

       a. hers is much more attractive

       b. your briefcase is much more attractive

       c. your briefcase isn't as attractive

17. A. Your furniture is more comfortable than mine.

    B. Don't be ridiculous! _____.

       a. Yours is much more comfortable than mine.

       b. Mine is much more comfortable than yours.

       c. Yours isn't as comfortable as mine.

18. A. The parks _____ they used to be.

    B. I agree. They used to be cleaner.

       a. are as clean as

       b. are cleaner than

       c. aren't as clean as

19. A. Our new rug is much softer than our old rug.

    B. I think so, too. Our old rug _____ our new rug.

       a. wasn't as soft as

       b. was as soft as

       c. was much softer than

20. A. Tim's apartment isn't as nice as Tom's apartment.

    B. _____. In my opinion, Tom's apartment is much nicer than Tim's apartment.

       a. I don't think so.

       b. I think so, too.

       c. Don't be ridiculous!

WHICH WORD?

A. What do you think? (Should)   Might   Will   I move to Easterly or Westerly?

B. I think you should move to Easterly. The people in Easterly are

friendlier as   friendlier than   more friendlier as [21] the people in Westerly.

A. I agree   think so   disagree [22] . I think the people in Westerly are much friendlier.

B. Do you really think so?

A. Definitely! The people in Easterly aren't as nice as they used   were   have [23] to be.

B. I think so, too. But Westerly is as   isn't   isn't as [24] exciting as Easterly.

A. I agree. But I also think Westerly is more safe   safer   more nice [25] than Easterly.

Score: _____

Student's Name _____ I.D. Number _____

Course _____ Teacher _____ Date _____

WHICH WORD DOESN'T BELONG?

Example:

a. stubborn	b. lazy	c. mean	(d.) friendly

1. a. polite | b. talented | c. obnoxious | d. kind

2. a. honest | b. convenient | c. comfortable | d. rude

3. a. elegant | b. fashionable | c. sloppy | d. popular

4. a. handsome | b. boring | c. pretty | d. beautiful

5. a. ugly | b. dependable | c. reliable | d. powerful

CHOOSE

Example:

He's the _____ person I know.
a. most smart
(b.) smartest
c. smarter
d. most smartest

6. I think your grandmother is
_____.
a. most energetic
b. very energetic
c. the very energetic
d. the very most energetic

7. Linda is _____ student in the
school.
a. very talented
b. more talented
c. the most talented
d. a more talented

8. I think you're a very _____ person.
a. nice
b. nicer
c. nicest
d. most nice

9. Your friend Andrew is much _____ than
your brother.
a. the funniest
b. funniest
c. the funnier
d. funnier

10. In my opinion, my uncle is _____
person in my family.
a. most wonderful
b. the more wonderful
c. the most wonderful
d. more wonderful

CHOOSE

Example:

Julie buys new clothes every year. She's the most _____ person I know.

a. fashionable
b. honest
c. polite
d. sloppy

11. Laura always gives very nice presents to her friends. She's the _____ person I know.

   a. most convenient
   b. most generous
   c. meanest
   d. most helpful

12. Victor has a lot of friends. He's the _____ person at school.

   a. most popular
   b. rudest
   c. most lightweight
   d. most stubborn

13. Everyone always sleeps in Mr. Green's class. He's the most _____ teacher at school.

   a. patient
   b. energetic
   c. boring
   d. worst

14. Our neighbors play loud music all the time. They're the _____ people we know.

   a. obnoxious
   b. most stubborn
   c. laziest
   d. noisiest

15. Marvin never says "Thank you" or "You're welcome." He's the _____ person I know.

   a. rudest
   b. most polite
   c. cheapest
   d. nicest

CHOOSE

Example:

It's much _____ than my old computer.

(a.) more powerful
b. most powerful
c. powerful
d. powerfuller

16. Don't you have _____ one?

a. a more small
b. a smaller
c. a smallest
d. as small as

17. What's _____ city in your country?

a. exciting
b. the more exciting
c. most exciting
d. the most exciting

18. Swiss watches are the _____ watches in the world.

a. very reliable
b. most reliable
c. more reliable than
d. more reliable

19. This is _____ one we have.

a. the warmest
b. the warm
c. the warmer
d. as warmest as

20. My mother's recipe for cake is _____ than yours.

a. the best
b. best
c. better
d. as best

WHAT'S THE WORD?

cleaner	expensive	comfortable	most	tastiest	healthy

Charlie's Kitchen is the _____ most _____ popular restaurant in my city. It's

_____ **21** than the Continental Restaurant. It's comfortable, but it isn't as

_____ **22** as the Country Cafe. It's more _____ **23** than Rita's Restaurant.

The food at Charlie's Kitchen is _____ **24** and delicious. In fact, everybody says it's

the _____ **25** food in town.

Score: _____

Student's Name _____ I.D. Number _____

Course _____ Teacher _____ Date _____

WHERE IS IT?

Example:

_____ South Street and you'll see the bank on the right.

a. Walk up
b. Drive
c. Turn
d. See

1. Walk along Main Street and you'll see the video store _____.

   a. across from
   b. on the left
   c. next to
   d. between the park

2. _____ along Third Avenue to Newton Street and turn left.

   a. Walk up
   b. You'll see
   c. Turn
   d. Drive

3. Take the First Street Bus and _____ at River Road.

   a. drive
   b. walk
   c. get off
   d. get

4. You'll see the school _____ the museum and the post office.

   a. between
   b. next
   c. on the right
   d. along

5. The zoo is _____ the bus stop.

   a. between
   b. on
   c. at the corner
   d. across from

WHAT'S THE QUESTION?

Example:

Can you tell me how to get _____?

a. the toy store
(b.) there
c. from here
d. the easiest way

6. _____ you tell me how to get to the university?

a. Do
b. Can you
c. Are
d. Could

7. What's _____ way to get to the concert hall?

a. the busiest
b. the directest
c. the fastest
d. best

8. _____ tell me how to get to the airport?

a. You would please
b. Would you please
c. Excuse me
d. Could please

9. What's the best way to get to the bus station _____ here?

a. to
b. by
c. from
d. for

10. Can you tell me how to get to _____?

a. Bridge Street
b. ice cream shop
c. hospital
d. the Park Street

CHOOSE

Example:

Walk _____ Park Street to Rolling Pond.

a. to
b. along
c. between
d. next to

11. You'll see the hardware store _____ the right.

a. or
b. by
c. on
d. in

12. Take the subway and get off _____ Central Avenue.

a. at
b. along
c. in
d. to

13. You'll see the museum at the corner _____ Ninth Street and Madison Avenue.

a. off
b. to
c. from
d. of

14. The Oak Street bus stops next_____ the courthouse.

a. of
b. for
c. to
d. from

15. Walk up this street _____ the corner of Main Street and Park Avenue and turn right.

a. on
b. to
c. between
d. at

WHICH WAY?

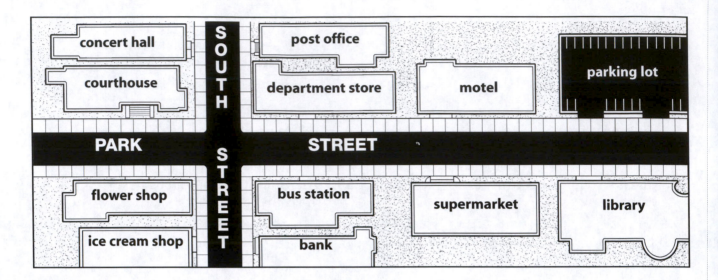

CHOOSE

Example:

Walk down South Street and
_____.

a. on the right
b.) turn right
c. see the flower shop
d. get off

16. Walk along Park Street and you'll see the parking lot _____ the library.

a. next to
b. on the left
c. across from
d. on the right

17. Walk up South Street. The post office is _____.

a. at the corner of
b. on the left
c. next to the courthouse
d. on the right

18. You'll see the supermarket _____ the bus station and the library.

a. between
b. across from
c. next
d. on the right

19. The _____ is at the corner of South Street and Park Street.

a. concert hall
b. bank
c. courthouse
d. ice cream shop

20. Walk down South Street and you'll see the ice cream shop _____.

a. on the right
b. at the corner of Park Street
c. on Park Street
d. up South Street

WHAT'S THE WORD?

of	on	to	at	from	off

It's easy to get to the park _____ *from* _____ here. Drive down this street _____ **21** the

corner _____ **22** First Avenue and Grant Street. Take the First Avenue Bus and get

_____ **23** _____ **24** Pine Street. You'll see the park _____ **25** the right, across

from the zoo.

Score: _____

Student's Name _____ I.D. Number _____

Course _____ Teacher _____ Date _____

CHOOSE

Example:

We need a _____ of ice cream.

a. jar
(b.) pint
c. pound
d. glass

1. He ate too _____ cheese.

   a. more
   b. much
   c. many
   d. few

2. It's going to rain. You _____ take a raincoat.

   a. don't
   b. can't
   c. should
   d. might not

3. If you walk _____ Main Street, you'll see the library across from the post office.

   a. off
   b. in
   c. at
   d. down

4. Sally _____ to the beach next week.

   a. went
   b. is going
   c. drove
   d. going

5. John is _____ than George.

   a. honester
   b. honest
   c. more honest
   d. as honest

6. The video store is _____ to the train station.

   a. across
   b. in front
   c. right
   d. next

7. Jim _____ his daughter to school every morning.

   a. going to drive
   b. is driving
   c. drives
   d. drive

8. Jane is _____ student in our class.

   a. the better
   b. the best
   c. as better as the
   d. best

9. _____ you tell me how to get to the ice cream shop?

   a. Could
   b. How
   c. Do
   d. Will you

10. How _____ does a bunch of grapes cost?

a. long
b. many
c. soon
d. much

11. What's _____ way to the book store?

a. easiest
b. fastest
c. the fastest
d. easiest

12. _____ the Pine Street bus to Fifth Street.

a. Take
b. Get off
c. Make
d. Took

13. My friend Betty _____ letters to her friend last weekend.

a. will be writing
b. wrote
c. writes
d. write

14. Howard's car isn't _____ Mike's car.

a. as expensive than
b. the most expensive as
c. as expensive as
d. the more expensive than

15. It's on the corner _____ Park Street and Ninth Avenue.

a. off
b. of
c. along
d. on

16. They _____ their car tomorrow.

a. going to wash
b. washed
c. washing
d. are going to wash

17. Pour in _____ water.

a. a box of
b. a pound of
c. a quart of
d. a little of

18. I'm afraid I _____ get hurt.

a. might
b. should
c. might not
d. am going

19. Let's buy a _____ of bread.

a. loaf
b. love
c. loaves
d. dozen

20. The movie will begin in _____.

a. eight thirty
b. fifteen minutes
c. few minutes
d. little while

21. Drive along South Street and _____ right at the restaurant.

a. on the
b. you're be
c. you'll see it
d. turn

22. Can I have a _____ pieces of pie?

   a. little

   b. few

   c. some

   d. not too many

23. This is the _____ one we have.

   a. large

   b. larger

   c. larger than the

   d. largest

24. There aren't _____ more strawberries.

   a. some

   b. much

   c. any

   d. as many

25. _____ be visiting you next Sunday.

   a. We'll

   b. We're

   c. Will

   d. We

26. There _____ any more lettuce.

   a. aren't

   b. shouldn't

   c. won't

   d. isn't

27. My classmates _____ to have a party next week.

   a. will

   b. might

   c. are going

   d. like

28. I need a _____ cereal.

   a. bag of

   b. bunch

   c. bowl

   d. box of

29. My sister is _____ than my brother.

   a. friendly

   b. as friendly as

   c. friendlier

   d. the friendlier

30. Sally's garden is more beautiful _____.

   a. than mine

   b. than my

   c. as mine

   d. as me

31. Did you _____ TV last night?

   a. saw him on

   b. wash

   c. watch

   d. watched

32. The game will end in _____.

   a. three o'clock

   b. few hours

   c. few minutes

   d. half an hour

33. When _____ here?

   a. will Bill be

   b. Bill will be

   c. will be Bill

   d. will be Bill be

34. We're afraid we _____ have a terrible time.

    a. don't

    b. won't

    c. might

    d. should

35. The bus stop is _____ the zoo.

    a. across from

    b. at the corner

    c. along

    d. between

36. Ann isn't as rich as Sue, but she's much _____.

    a. happiest

    b. as happy

    c. happy

    d. happier

37. What are you _____ now?

    a. doing

    b. going

    c. do

    d. study in school

38. I _____ a sweater for his birthday last year.

    a. give him

    b. him gave

    c. gave him

    d. gave him to

39. Do the monkeys _____ eat bananas?

    a. want

    b. like to

    c. usual

    d. like

40. _____ the soup be ready soon?

    a. Does

    b. Is

    c. Will

    d. Do

WHICH WORD?

Ralph wants [buy (to buy) buys] [some   many   few]⁴¹ new clothes,

so on Saturday he's [go   going   will]⁴² to the department store downtown. Last

summer Ralph [buys   buyed   bought]⁴³ a [few   little   many]⁴⁴ pairs of

pants, but this year he isn't as [thin   thinner   thinnest]⁴⁵ as he was before.

Ralph also wants to buy a new TV. He has a nice TV now, but he wants to buy

[nicest   the most nice   the nicest]⁴⁶ TV available. He [likes   might   will]⁴⁷

buy the TV at the department store, but there's a [good   the best   best]⁴⁸ TV store

[next   around   across]⁴⁹ from the department store. Maybe [will   he'll   he's]⁵⁰

buy the TV at the department store, and maybe he won't.

Score: _____

Student's Name _____ I.D. Number _____

Course _____ Teacher _____ Date _____

CHOOSE

Example:

Barbara dances _____.

a. graceful
b. slow
c. bad
(d.) gracefully

1. Mr. Lee is a very _____ translator.

a. accurate
b. slowly
c. well
d. accurately

2. Your friend Ron doesn't drive very _____.

a. good
b. careless
c. carefully
d. careful

3. Nancy is a _____ piano player.

a. accurate
b. beautiful
c. badly
d. beautifully

4. Mr. Jones used to be a good teacher, but now he teaches _____.

a. good
b. well
c. bad
d. badly

5. Jim has nice clothes, but he dresses _____.

a. sloppy
b. bad
c. sloppily
d. careless

CHOOSE

Example:

Those painters paint very carelessly. They should paint more _____.

a. carelessly
b. neater
c. quick
(d.) carefully

6. Jane always goes to bed too late. She should go to bed _____.

a. more lately
b. earlier
c. more early
d. later

7. William speaks very impolitely. He should speak more _____.

a. loudly
b. better
c. politely
d. well

8. Stella is a terrible student. She should study _____.

a. more harder
b. more terribly
c. more hardly
d. harder

9. Joe cooks very badly. He should try to cook _____.

a. more well
b. better
c. more good
d. worse

10. Andrew drives very fast. He should try to drive _____.

a. more slowly
b. more quicker
c. more faster
d. more slow

CHOOSE

Example:

If Barbara _____ a new car, _____ have much money left.

a. will buy . . . she'll
b. buys . . . she won't
c. buys . . . she'll have
d. will buy . . . she won't

11. If Roger _____ his rent, his landlord _____ him.

a. won't pay . . . won't evict
b. doesn't pay . . . will evict
c. pays . . . will evict
d. won't pay . . . will evict

12. If Patty _____ to school tomorrow, _____ the bus.

a. doesn't walk . . . she'll take
b. walks . . . she'll take
c. walks . . . she takes
d. doesn't walk . . . she takes

13. If _____, James _____ his raincoat.

a. it doesn't rain . . . will wear
b. it will rain . . . will wear
c. it rains . . . will wear
d. it won't rain . . . won't wear

14. If the teacher _____ us a lot of homework, _____ stay up late.

a. will give . . . we'll have to
b. gives . . . we won't have to
c. will give . . . we have to
d. gives . . . we'll have to

15. If they _____ good food, _____ to the party.

a. don't have . . . I won't go
b. might have . . . I won't go
c. have . . . I go
d. will have . . . I'll go

CHOOSE

Example:

If you drive too fast, you might _____.

a. get a sore throat
b. have an accident *(circled)*
c. be tired
d. be quiet

16. If they listen to loud music, they might hurt their _____.

a. a CD player
b. ears
c. eyes
d. throat

17. If Larry always gets to work late, he might get _____.

a. a backache
b. a raise
c. fired
d. tired

18. If I eat too quickly, I might get _____.

a. a headache
b. a sore throat
c. tired
d. a stomachache

19. If you don't go to bed early, you might _____.

a. be late for school
b. have nightmares
c. go to bed late
d. be early for the meeting

20. If Carl doesn't give his girlfriend a birthday present, she might _____.

a. evict him
b. go back to school
c. be angry
d. lose his job

WHICH WORD?

My brother-in-law Richard works too [(slowly)   quick   slow]. I think he should

work [more fast   more quickly   more faster]²¹. If he does that, his supervisor

[might not   should   shouldn't]²² fire him. I also think Richard

[might   shouldn't   won't]²³ come to work so [lately   later   late]²⁴. If he

[will come   comes   will arrive]²⁵ to work on time, he might not lose his job.

Score: _____

| Student's Name | | I.D. Number |
| Course | Teacher | Date |

CHOOSE

Example:

Yesterday at 2:30 _____ dinner.

  (a.) I was cooking
  b. I'll cook
  c. I'm cooking
  d. was I cooking

1. I saw your brother. _____ out of the library.

  a. He was walked
  b. He's walking
  c. He was walking
  d. He walking

2. I saw you and Jack yesterday. _____ through the park.

  a. They were jogging
  b. You were jogging
  c. You're jogging
  d. You'll jog

3. _____ Mrs. Park _____ her sink?

  a. Was . . . fixed
  b. Did . . . fixing
  c. Were . . . fixing
  d. Was . . . fixing

4. I saw Susan and her children. They _____ at the beach.

  a. were swimming
  b. swimming
  c. swam
  d. was swimming

5. _____ you studying when I called?

  a. Are
  b. Were
  c. Was
  d. Did

WHAT HAPPENED?

Example:

Jane tripped while she _____ down the stairs.

- a. walked
- (b.) was walking
- c. walks
- d. walked out

6. A dog _____ Brian while he was walking to school.

- a. was biting
- b. bit
- c. bites
- d. bited

7. While he _____, Mr. Jackson cut himself.

- a. shaves
- b. shaved
- c. was shaving
- d. shaving

8. A thief broke into our apartment while _____.

- a. we shop
- b. we did shop
- c. did we shop
- d. we were shopping

9. _____ you burn yourself while you were cooking dinner?

- a. Should
- b. Did
- c. Are
- d. Were

10. Lucy and Tommy _____ while they were getting off the bus.

- a. tripped and fell
- b. were tripped and falling
- c. trip and fell
- d. were tripping and fall

CHOOSE

Example:

My nephew went to the movies by _____.

- a. hisself
- (b.) himself
- c. herself

11. James and Diane ate dinner by _____.

- a. theirselves
- b. themselves
- c. ourselves

12. You'll have to go jogging by _____.

- a. yourselves
- b. youself
- c. myself

13. My friends and I have to take the subway by _____.

- a. myself
- b. ourselfs
- c. ourselves

14. My niece does her homework by _____.

- a. herself
- b. herselves
- c. himself

15. I don't like to drive at night by _____.

- a. meself
- b. myself
- c. yourself

CHOOSE

Example:

Which apartment _____ you live in?

a. are
(b.) do
c. were
d. does

16. What _____ you doing last night at 7:00?

a. are
b. was
c. were
d. did

17. Who _____ you go swimming with yesterday afternoon?

a. does
b. did
c. do
d. will

18. What did your daughter _____?

a. doing
b. did
c. go
d. do

19. What was he _____ for lunch?

a. making
b. make
c. made
d. eat

20. Did you _____ when you saw the accident?

a. fainting
b. called
c. faint
d. fainted

WHAT'S THE WORD?

himself	shouting	saw	was	while	were

On Saturdays, Frank likes to take a walk downtown by ___himself___. Last weekend

_____ 21 he was walking down Park Avenue, he _____ 22 an accident. A man in a

black sports car _____ 23 driving too fast, and he crashed into a truck. The man and the

truck driver _____ 24 very upset. They were _____ 25 at each other for a long time.

Score: _____

Student's Name _____ I.D. Number _____

Course _____ Teacher _____ Date _____

CHOOSE

Example:

Sam _____ play basketball because he was too short.

a. can't
(b.) couldn't
c. wasn't able
d. could

1. I'm happy I _____ play the piano beautifully now.

a. can
b. can't
c. couldn't
d. are able

2. He _____ go to work yesterday because he was sick.

a. can't
b. could
c. wasn't able
d. couldn't

3. Nancy _____ to do the homework because it was too difficult.

a. won't be able
b. couldn't
c. wasn't able
d. was able

4. I'm sorry. I _____ speak Spanish very well.

a. am able
b. can't
c. can
d. able to

5. When I was young I _____ talk to girls because I was too shy.

a. can't
b. was able to
c. could
d. couldn't

6. I'm sure I _____ be able to fall asleep tonight.

a. wasn't
b. won't
c. can't
d. not

7. _____ your sister able to go to the concert?

a. Was
b. Were
c. Will
d. Does

8. I _____ able to do the math homework today.

a. can't be
b. won't
c. not
d. wasn't

9. _____ your cats able to eat dinner on time?

    a. Have

    b. Will

    c. Were

    d. Can

10. Mr. Jackson _____ be able to call you this weekend.

    a. was

    b. can't

    c. can

    d. won't

CHOOSE

Example:

_____ got to go to work now.

    (a.) I've

    b. I had

    c. I'll

    d. I'm

11. _____ got to do their homework.

    a. They'll

    b. They had

    c. They've

    d. They

12. _____ to take my wife to the hospital.

    a. I had

    b. I've

    c. I've got to

    d. I got

13. _____ to study for a test.

    a. She's

    b. She has to

    c. She had

    d. She need

14. _____ have to eat dinner by yourself.

    a. You've

    b. You've got to

    c. You got to

    d. You'll

15. _____ got to go to baseball practice.

    a. We

    b. We've

    c. We had

    d. We'll

CHOOSE

Example:

I couldn't go to lunch with my friends because I was too _____.

a. young
b. busy
c. cold
d. difficult

16. Michael couldn't perform in his piano recital because he was too _____.

a. shy
b. spicy
c. crowded
d. disappointed

17. I couldn't lift the box because it was too _____.

a. small
b. weak
c. heavy
d. frustrated

18. They couldn't solve the math problem because it was too _____.

a. nervous
b. upset
c. full
d. difficult

19. We couldn't finish our dinner because we were too _____.

a. hungry
b. full
c. short
d. tall

20. Susie couldn't swim this afternoon because she was too _____.

a. windy
b. crowded
c. tired
d. warm

WHICH WORD?

A. Hello. You [have   should   got] to send someone to fix my kitchen sink. There's

water everywhere, and I've [can't   have   got]²¹ to get to work!

B. I'm sorry. I [can't   have to   able]²² send a repairperson right now. We're very

[difficult   busy   heavy]²³ today. We [got   going   have]²⁴ to fix a lot of sinks.

I won't [can't   able to   be able]²⁵ to send a repairperson for a few more hours.

Score: _____

Student's Name	I.D. Number
Course	Teacher	Date

CHOOSE

Example:

Henry is a little too heavy. He must eat _____ potato chips.

a. more
(b.) fewer
c. less

1. Ron wants to lose weight. He should eat _____ fatty meat.

a. more
b. fewer
c. less

2. Harold is a little overweight. His doctor says he must eat _____ vegetables and other good foods.

a. more
b. fewer
c. less

3. My grandmother has to lose some weight. She has to eat _____ cookies.

a. more
b. fewer
c. less

4. If you're overweight, you should eat less candy and _____ fruit.

a. more
b. fewer
c. less

5. Stan is a little heavy. He must eat _____ rich desserts.

a. more
b. fewer
c. less

CHOOSE

Example:

I _____ eat as much ice cream as I did before.

(a.) mustn't
b. have to
c. don't have to
d. am able

6. Here at the ABC Company, you _____ come to work late.

a. don't have to
b. have to
c. mustn't
d. must

7. Men _____ wear a necktie every day at our company.

a. got to
b. don't have to
c. not able to
d. mustn't

8. At our school, we _____ speak rudely to anyone.

a. have to
b. must
c. don't have to
d. mustn't

9. Jim is heavy. He _____ go on a diet.

a. mustn't
b. doesn't have to
c. has to
d. able to

10. You _____ be careless when you're driving.

a. have to
b. must
c. mustn't
d. don't have to

CHOOSE

Example:

I had a complete _____ yesterday.

a. health
b. examination (circled)
c. diet
d. instruction

11. The doctor used _____ to listen to my heart.

a. a chest X-ray
b. a stethoscope
c. electrical wiring
d. a pulse

12. The nurse took my _____.

a. scale
b. checkup
c. blood pressure
d. blood test

13. He talked with me about my _____.

a. weight
b. overweight
c. technician
d. medical

14. The doctor says I have a strong _____.

a. weight
b. blood
c. height
d. heart

15. Then I stood on _____.

a. a cardiogram
b. a scale
c. an X-ray
d. my chest

CHOOSE

Example:

My parents told me I _____ study because I have a test tomorrow.

a. must (circled)
b. don't have to
c. will
d. mustn't

16. If you have a cold, you _____ drink some hot tea.

a. mustn't
b. will
c. should
d. don't

17. Our landlord said we _____ make noise because the neighbors will be upset.

a. might
b. mustn't
c. must
d. should

18. She _____ go to the party because she has to work overtime.

a. must
b. mustn't
c. doesn't have to
d. can't

19. Gloria _____ stop eating spicy food or she's going to have stomach problems.

    a. mustn't

    b. might

    c. must

    d. will

20. If you get to work late every day, your boss _____ get angry.

    a. must

    b. might

    c. doesn't

    d. shouldn't

WHICH WORD?

A. I'm really worried about your heart, Mr. Tyler.

B. What [could   couldn't   (should)] I do, Dr. Blake?

A. You [must   shouldn't   mustn't]²¹ eat [fewer   less   more]²² cake and [fewer   too many   less]²³ french fries.

B. I see. And should I stop eating candy?

A. No. You [mustn't   should   don't have to]²⁴ stop eating candy, but you [can   mustn't   have to]²⁵ eat as much as you did before.

Score: _____

| Student's Name | _____ | I.D. Number | _____ |
| Course | _____ | Teacher | _____ | Date | _____ |

CHOOSE

Example:

He'll _____ his floors today.

(a.) be mopping
b. will mop
c. mopping
d. won't mop

1. _____ be rearranging furniture tonight.

a. She
b. She's
c. She'll
d. Will

2. _____ be home tonight. I'll be visiting my grandparents.

a. I'll be
b. I won't
c. I'll be being
d. I'm

3. _____ mittens this evening.

a. He'll be knitting
b. She'll be sitting
c. I'll be bathing
d. They'll be repainting

4. I'm sure _____ call us soon.

a. they'll be
b. they're
c. they
d. they'll

5. We'll be home all evening. _____ bills.

a. We pay
b. We'll pay
c. We'll be paying
d. We're be paying

WHAT'S THE QUESTION?

Example:

Will you _____ busy this evening?

a. be
b. being
c. are
d. will be

6. How _____ will you be bathing the dog?

a. much
b. soon
c. far
d. longer

7. How late _____ you be working tonight?

a. do
b. until
c. are
d. will

8. When can you _____ to the store?

a. be going
b. going
c. go
d. will be going

9. How _____ will you be staying at the party?

a. long
b. longer
c. much
d. soon

10. How much _____ will you be exercising?

a. long
b. sooner
c. longer
d. late

CHOOSE

Example:

I'll be working on my car _____ another half hour.

a. until
b. for *(circled)*
c. at
d. an

11. I'll be staying here _____ a few more days.

a. for
b. until
c. at
d. from

12. We won't be arriving _____ next week.

a. for
b. until
c. in
d. at

13. Uncle George will be arriving _____ a few days.

a. until
b. to
c. at
d. in

14. We'll be driving _____ a few more hours.

a. from
b. until
c. for
d. at

15. Jane will be studying _____ 10 o'clock.

a. for
b. in
c. of
d. at

WHAT'S THE RESPONSE?

Example:

When can you come over?

(a.) At 5 o'clock.

b. Until tomorrow.

c. For three hours.

d. A week.

16. May I speak to Carol?

a. That'll be fine.

b. Hold on a moment.

c. Yes, you will.

d. That's okay.

17. Hello. This is Diane.

a. Hi, Diane! I'll see you then.

b. Do you want to speak to Diane?

c. Hi, Diane! How are you?

d. Hello. Is this Diane?

18. Can I take a message?

a. I'm not here right now.

b. Don't worry. You can take it.

c. You're welcome.

d. Please tell George that Chris called.

19. How about 8 o'clock?

a. I'll be glad to help you.

b. That'll be fine.

c. Yes, I will.

d. What is it about?

20. Will you be home on Saturday?

a. Yes, I will. I'll be sewing.

b. Yes, I will. I'll be driving.

c. No, I won't. I'll be home.

d. Yes, I will. I'll be growing up.

WHICH WORD?

A. When (will) is until your sister be arriving?

B. She'll be | arrive   get here   arriving |²¹ | for   in   until |²² a few hours.

A. How long will she be staying with us?

B. She wants to stay | until   for   to |²³ next Friday.

A. What | she'll be   will she'll be   will she be |²⁴ doing while she's here?

B. I think | will she be   she be   she'll be |²⁵ looking for a job.

Score: _____

Student's Name _____ I.D. Number _____

Course _____ Teacher _____ Date _____

CHOOSE

Example:

I always like to eat the _____.

- (a.) chef's stew
- b. chefs stew
- c. stew of the chef
- d. stew of the chef's

1. This must be _____ notebook.

- a. my sons
- b. Georges'
- c. a students'
- d. a student's

2. I don't agree with those _____ opinions.

- a. teacher's
- b. mechanics'
- c. peoples
- d. students

3. Where should I put this _____ information.

- a. doctors'
- b. patients'
- c. patient's
- d. patients

4. Charlie is our _____ son.

- a. friend
- b. superintendent's
- c. friends
- d. superintendents'

5. My _____ homework is very difficult.

- a. daughters
- b. childrens'
- c. teacher
- d. children's

CHOOSE

Example:

I don't know _____ about washing machines.

a. something
(b.) anything
c. somebody

6. _____ cleaned all the dishes.

a. Did anyone
b. Anybody
c. Somebody

7. There isn't _____ at the door.

a. someone
b. anyone
c. something

8. Do you know _____ who can play the drums?

a. anything
b. something
c. anyone

9. I hope _____ comes to our party.

a. somebody
b. anybody
c. some people

10. If I don't study, I won't understand _____ on the test.

a. anyone
b. any questions
c. something

CHOOSE

Example:

His family didn't help _____.

a. his
b. himself
(c.) him
d. your

11. We don't have to mop the floor by _____.

a. us
b. ourselves
c. ourself
d. ourselfs

12. She didn't eat _____ breakfast.

a. herself
b. him
c. hers
d. her

13. I don't think these shirts are _____.

a. them
b. there's
c. theirs
d. their's

14. He finished his homework, and I finished _____.

a. mine
b. his
c. myself
d. my

15. Bob, can you iron your clothes by _____?

a. himself
b. yourself
c. your
d. youself

CHOOSE

Example:

My next-door neighbors _____ arguing last night.

a. will be
b. (were)
c. are
d. didn't be

16. The weather last weekend was terrible. It _____ all weekend.

a. will be raining
b. might rain
c. rained
d. raining

17. The mechanic always _____ a long time to arrive.

a. takes
b. is taking
c. was taking
d. take

18. How much longer _____ rearranging your furniture?

a. will be you
b. are you be
c. will you be
d. can be

19. I'll _____ my garage all day Sunday.

a. am cleaning
b. cleaning
c. might clean
d. be cleaning

20. She was repainting the kitchen when her mother _____.

a. was arriving
b. arrived
c. will be arriving
d. is going to arrive

WHICH WORD?

A. There's [anything (something) somebody] wrong with my bathtub. Can you send a

[locksmith   repair   plumber]²¹ to fix it as soon as possible?

B. I can send [someone   body   anyone]²² there tomorrow morning.

[Does that   Is that   Are you]²³ okay?

A. I'm afraid I won't be home then. I'll [work   working   be working]²⁴ .

B. How about tomorrow afternoon?

A. [That'll   That   That's]²⁵ be fine.

Score: _____

Student's Name _____ I.D. Number _____

Course _____ Teacher _____ Date _____

CHOOSE

Example:

I've _____ to work all day this Saturday.

a. must
b. have
c. got *(circled)*
d. going

1. My brother Marty plays the piano _____.

a. more terrible
b. terribly
c. the most terrible
d. very bad

2. Susan _____ when the lights went out.

a. reads
b. read
c. is reading
d. was reading

3. _____ sewing at five o'clock tomorrow.

a. I'll be
b. I'm going to
c. I might
d. I was

4. If Sam eats his dinner, he _____ be hungry later.

a. could
b. doesn't
c. won't
d. should

5. My children and I enjoyed _____ at the beach.

a. themselves
b. ourselves
c. theirselves
d. myself

6. I don't think there's _____ who can drive me to school.

a. somebody
b. something
c. anybody
d. someone

7. If you speak too _____, no one will be able to understand you.

a. fast
b. faster
c. fastly
d. longly

8. Grandpa _____ go to the picnic because he was too tired.

a. can't
b. couldn't
c. shouldn't
d. had to

9. My doctor says I should eat _____ spicy food.

a. fewer
b. a few
c. less
d. many

10. The electrician's prices are usually very _____.

a. reasonably
b. more reasonable
c. most reasonable
d. reasonable

11. My niece hurt her leg while she _____ tennis.

a. played
b. plays
c. was playing
d. will be playing

12. Barry _____ stop eating fatty foods because he's a little heavy.

a. going to
b. must
c. doesn't have to
d. mustn't

13. I think you should try to drive _____.

a. more carefully
b. more careful
c. too carefully
d. carefuller

14. Marvin _____ go to work because he was sick.

a. had to
b. wanted to
c. could
d. wasn't able to

15. My husband will _____ talking on the phone for a while.

a. is
b. going to be
c. be
d. might be

16. That isn't his cell phone. It's _____.

a. my
b. mine
c. him
d. me

17. My brother and I walk _____ the park every day.

a. down
b. up
c. through
d. at

18. Can you do your homework by _____?

a. myself
b. yourselves
c. ourselves
d. youself

19. He _____ to speak English perfectly.

a. will be able
b. might
c. should
d. was able to

20. If you want to keep this job, you _____ get to work on time.

a. mustn't
b. shouldn't
c. don't have to
d. have to

21. How much longer _____ chatting online?

a. will be he
b. will he be
c. he will be
d. is he be

22. I won't go to college _____ four more years.

   a. until

   b. at

   c. for

   d. from

23. While he was playing basketball, _____ to rain.

   a. it's starting

   b. it started

   c. it starts

   d. it'll be starting

24. If it _____ snow, my grandmother will take a walk today.

   a. will

   b. won't

   c. doesn't

   d. will not

25. _____ you tell me how to get to the post office?

   a. Could

   b. Should

   c. Must

   d. Do

26. I have to lose weight. My doctor says I _____ eat fatty foods.

   a. should

   b. mustn't

   c. have to

   d. want to

27. We won't be at the game _____ six thirty.

   a. for

   b. in

   c. until

   d. to

28. Do you know _____ good electricians?

   a. any

   b. anybody

   c. anyone

   d. someone

29. When I was a teenager, I never _____ TV.

   a. was watching

   b. will watch

   c. watch

   d. watched

30. Mario _____ when the phone rang.

   a. was vacuuming

   b. vacuumed

   c. vacuums

   d. was vacuumed

31. I have to eat _____ spicy food.

   a. a few

   b. fewer

   c. less

   d. much

32. The nurse _____ my blood pressure.

   a. did

   b. had

   c. stood

   d. took

33. If he _____ basketball too often, he might hurt his knees.

   a. practice

   b. practices

   c. practicing

   d. will be practicing

34. Is this wallet _____?

   a. you

   b. your

   c. yours

   d. yous

35. Get _____ the bus at First Street.

   a. off

   b. of

   c. for

   d. to

36. I'm sorry. We _____ be able to come to your party on Saturday.

   a. might

   b. can't

   c. won't

   d. must

37. My new computer wasn't too _____.

   a. expensive

   b. expensively

   c. much expensive

   d. most expensive

38. How much longer _____ my mother be working?

   a. does

   b. are

   c. was

   d. will

39. You _____ speak impolitely to your boss.

   a. mustn't

   b. don't have to

   c. have to

   d. should

40. Mary can't come to the meeting. She's _____ take her husband to the hospital.

   a. has to

   b. going

   c. will

   d. got to

WHICH WORD?

Jack is a very good plumber. He always (helps)   helping   helped   people

quick   quickly   fastly   **41** , and he doesn't charge them   many   much   little   **42**

money. Last week   while   who   how   **43**   Ethel   will be   is   was   **44**

washing the dishes, she saw something wrong with her sink. She called Jack, and he was there

in   for   until   **45**   thirty minutes.   Where   While   When   **46**   he arrived, he

was able   had   could   **47**   to repair the sink very quickly.

So, if you don't know   something   anyone   anything   **48**   about plumbing, you

shouldn't   couldn't   must   **49**   try to fix a problem by   youself   yourself   itself   **50** .

You should call Jack, the plumber.

Score: _____

CHAPTER 1

CHOOSE

1. d
2. c
3. b
4. b
5. a

CHOOSE

6. c
7. a
8. d
9. c
10. b

CHOOSE

11. b
12. c
13. d
14. c
15. a
16. d
17. b
18. c
19. a
20. c

WHICH WORD?

21. went
22. work
23. Last
24. her
25. likes to

CHAPTER 2

CHOOSE

1. c
2. d
3. a
4. b
5. c

CHOOSE

6. b
7. d
8. a
9. c
10. b

CHOOSE

11. a
12. c
13. d
14. b
15. c

CHOOSE

16. c
17. b
18. d
19. a
20. d

WHAT'S THE WORD?

21. are
22. they
23. it
24. much
25. is

CHAPTER 3

CHOOSE

1. b
2. c
3. a
4. d
5. c

CHOOSE

6. b
7. d
8. a
9. c
10. b

CHOOSE

11. c
12. b
13. a
14. d
15. c

CHOOSE

16. b
17. c
18. a
19. d
20. b

WHAT'S THE WORD?

21. pint
22. of
23. It
24. lot
25. is

CHAPTER 4

CHOOSE

1. c
2. d
3. a
4. b
5. c

WHEN?

6. c
7. b
8. d
9. a
10. c

CHOOSE

11. b
12. c
13. d
14. b
15. a

CHOOSE

16. c
17. b
18. d
19. a
20. b

WHICH WORD?

21. might
22. Are you
23. might
24. Will
25. might

CHAPTER 5

CHOOSE

1. c
2. b
3. d
4. a
5. a
6. b
7. d
8. a
9. c
10. b

CHOOSE

11. d
12. a
13. b
14. c
15. d

OPINIONS

16. b
17. a
18. c
19. a
20. b

WHICH WORD?

21. friendlier than
22. disagree
23. used
24. isn't as
25. safer

CHAPTER 6

WHICH WORD DOESN'T BELONG?

1. c
2. d
3. c
4. b
5. a

CHOOSE

6. b
7. c
8. a
9. d
10. c

CHOOSE

11. b
12. a
13. c
14. d
15. a

CHOOSE

16. b
17. d
18. b
19. a
20. c

WHAT'S THE WORD?

21. cleaner
22. comfortable
23. expensive
24. healthy
25. tastiest

CHAPTER 7

WHERE IS IT?

1. b
2. d
3. c
4. a
5. d

WHAT'S THE QUESTION?

6. d
7. c
8. b
9. c
10. a

CHOOSE

11. c
12. a
13. d
14. c
15. b

WHICH WAY?

16. c
17. d
18. a
19. c
20. a

WHAT'S THE WORD?

21. to
22. of
23. off
24. at
25. on

MID-BOOK TEST

CHOOSE

1. b
2. c
3. d
4. b
5. c
6. d
7. c
8. b
9. a
10. d
11. c
12. a
13. b
14. c
15. b
16. d
17. c
18. a
19. a
20. b
21. d
22. b
23. d
24. c
25. a
26. d
27. c
28. d
29. c
30. a
31. c
32. d
33. a
34. c
35. a
36. d
37. a
38. c
39. b
40. c

WHICH WORD?

41. some
42. going
43. bought
44. few
45. thin
46. the nicest
47. might
48. good
49. across
50. he'll

CHAPTER 8

CHOOSE

1. a
2. c
3. b
4. d
5. c

CHOOSE

6. b
7. c
8. d
9. b
10. a

CHOOSE

11. b
12. a
13. c
14. d
15. a

CHOOSE

16. b
17. c
18. d
19. a
20. c

WHICH WORD?

21. more quickly
22. might not
23. shouldn't
24. late
25. comes

CHAPTER 9

CHOOSE

1. c
2. b
3. d
4. a
5. b

WHAT HAPPENED?

6. b
7. c
8. d
9. b
10. a

CHOOSE

11. b
12. a
13. c
14. a
15. b

CHOOSE

16. c
17. b
18. d
19. a
20. c

WHAT'S THE WORD?

21. while
22. saw
23. was
24. were
25. shouting

CHAPTER 10

CHOOSE

1. a
2. d
3. c
4. b
5. d
6. b
7. a
8. d
9. c
10. d

CHOOSE

11. c
12. a
13. c
14. d
15. b

CHOOSE

16. a   19. b
17. c   20. c
18. d

WHICH WORD?

21. got
22. can't
23. busy
24. have
25. be able

CHAPTER 11

CHOOSE

1. c   4. a
2. a   5. b
3. b

CHOOSE

6. c   9. c
7. b   10. c
8. d

CHOOSE

11. b   14. d
12. c   15. b
13. a

CHOOSE

16. c   19. c
17. b   20. b
18. d

WHICH WORD?

21. must
22. less
23. fewer
24. don't have to
25. mustn't

CHAPTER 12

CHOOSE

1. c   4. d
2. b   5. c
3. a

WHAT'S THE QUESTION?

6. b   9. a
7. d   10. c
8. c

CHOOSE

11. a   14. c
12. b   15. d
13. d

WHAT'S THE RESPONSE?

16. b   19. b
17. c   20. a
18. d

WHICH WORD?

21. arriving
22. in
23. until
24. will she be
25. she'll be

CHAPTER 13

CHOOSE

1. d   4. b
2. b   5. d
3. c

CHOOSE

6. c   9. a
7. b   10. b
8. c

CHOOSE

11. b   14. a
12. d   15. b
13. c

CHOOSE

16. c   19. d
17. a   20. b
18. c

WHICH WORD?

21. plumber
22. someone
23. Is that
24. be working
25. That'll

FINAL TEST

CHOOSE

1. b   21. b
2. d   22. c
3. a   23. b
4. c   24. c
5. b   25. a
6. c   26. b
7. a   27. c
8. b   28. a
9. c   29. d
10. d   30. a
11. c   31. c
12. b   32. d
13. a   33. b
14. d   34. c
15. c   35. a
16. b   36. c
17. c   37. a
18. b   38. d
19. a   39. a
20. d   40. d

WHICH WORD?

41. quickly   46. When
42. much   47. was able
43. while   48. anything
44. was   49. shouldn't
45. in   50. yourself

SIDE BY SIDE
Chapter Test Answer Sheet

BOOK _____

CHAPTER _____

Student's Name _____   I.D. Number _____

Course _____   Teacher _____   Date _____

1 Ⓐ Ⓑ Ⓒ Ⓓ   11 Ⓐ Ⓑ Ⓒ Ⓓ

2 Ⓐ Ⓑ Ⓒ Ⓓ   12 Ⓐ Ⓑ Ⓒ Ⓓ

3 Ⓐ Ⓑ Ⓒ Ⓓ   13 Ⓐ Ⓑ Ⓒ Ⓓ

4 Ⓐ Ⓑ Ⓒ Ⓓ   14 Ⓐ Ⓑ Ⓒ Ⓓ

5 Ⓐ Ⓑ Ⓒ Ⓓ   15 Ⓐ Ⓑ Ⓒ Ⓓ

6 Ⓐ Ⓑ Ⓒ Ⓓ   16 Ⓐ Ⓑ Ⓒ Ⓓ

7 Ⓐ Ⓑ Ⓒ Ⓓ   17 Ⓐ Ⓑ Ⓒ Ⓓ

8 Ⓐ Ⓑ Ⓒ Ⓓ   18 Ⓐ Ⓑ Ⓒ Ⓓ

9 Ⓐ Ⓑ Ⓒ Ⓓ   19 Ⓐ Ⓑ Ⓒ Ⓓ

10 Ⓐ Ⓑ Ⓒ Ⓓ   20 Ⓐ Ⓑ Ⓒ Ⓓ

21 _____

22 _____

23 _____

24 _____

25 _____

SIDE BY SIDE
Mid-Book & Final Test Answer Sheet

BOOK _____

Check One:
☐ MID-BOOK TEST
☐ FINAL TEST

Student's Name _____   I.D. Number _____

Course _____   Teacher _____   Date _____

1 Ⓐ Ⓑ Ⓒ Ⓓ   11 Ⓐ Ⓑ Ⓒ Ⓓ   21 Ⓐ Ⓑ Ⓒ Ⓓ   31 Ⓐ Ⓑ Ⓒ Ⓓ
2 Ⓐ Ⓑ Ⓒ Ⓓ   12 Ⓐ Ⓑ Ⓒ Ⓓ   22 Ⓐ Ⓑ Ⓒ Ⓓ   32 Ⓐ Ⓑ Ⓒ Ⓓ
3 Ⓐ Ⓑ Ⓒ Ⓓ   13 Ⓐ Ⓑ Ⓒ Ⓓ   23 Ⓐ Ⓑ Ⓒ Ⓓ   33 Ⓐ Ⓑ Ⓒ Ⓓ
4 Ⓐ Ⓑ Ⓒ Ⓓ   14 Ⓐ Ⓑ Ⓒ Ⓓ   24 Ⓐ Ⓑ Ⓒ Ⓓ   34 Ⓐ Ⓑ Ⓒ Ⓓ
5 Ⓐ Ⓑ Ⓒ Ⓓ   15 Ⓐ Ⓑ Ⓒ Ⓓ   25 Ⓐ Ⓑ Ⓒ Ⓓ   35 Ⓐ Ⓑ Ⓒ Ⓓ
6 Ⓐ Ⓑ Ⓒ Ⓓ   16 Ⓐ Ⓑ Ⓒ Ⓓ   26 Ⓐ Ⓑ Ⓒ Ⓓ   36 Ⓐ Ⓑ Ⓒ Ⓓ
7 Ⓐ Ⓑ Ⓒ Ⓓ   17 Ⓐ Ⓑ Ⓒ Ⓓ   27 Ⓐ Ⓑ Ⓒ Ⓓ   37 Ⓐ Ⓑ Ⓒ Ⓓ
8 Ⓐ Ⓑ Ⓒ Ⓓ   18 Ⓐ Ⓑ Ⓒ Ⓓ   28 Ⓐ Ⓑ Ⓒ Ⓓ   38 Ⓐ Ⓑ Ⓒ Ⓓ
9 Ⓐ Ⓑ Ⓒ Ⓓ   19 Ⓐ Ⓑ Ⓒ Ⓓ   29 Ⓐ Ⓑ Ⓒ Ⓓ   39 Ⓐ Ⓑ Ⓒ Ⓓ
10 Ⓐ Ⓑ Ⓒ Ⓓ   20 Ⓐ Ⓑ Ⓒ Ⓓ   30 Ⓐ Ⓑ Ⓒ Ⓓ   40 Ⓐ Ⓑ Ⓒ Ⓓ

41 _____

42 _____

43 _____

44 _____

45 _____

46 _____

47 _____

48 _____

49 _____

50 _____

Duplication for classroom use is permitted.